LETTERS MAKE W

b
r
i
d
y
a
l
d

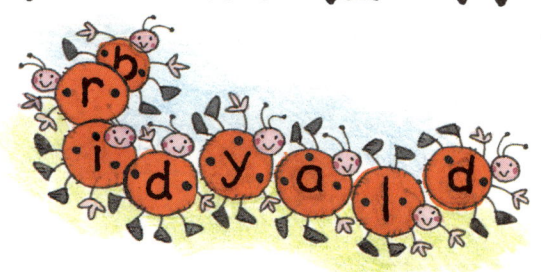

Unjumble these groups of letters to make words. Look at the pictures.

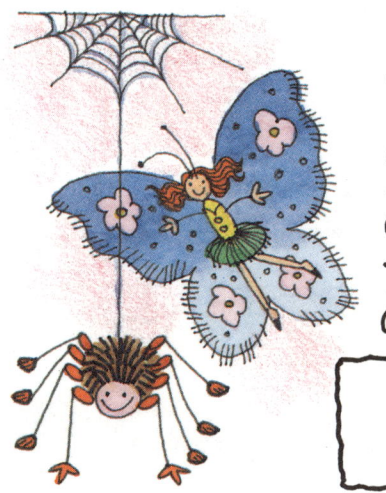

tna
pdisre
bridyald
etelbe
fulbetytr
detcenipe

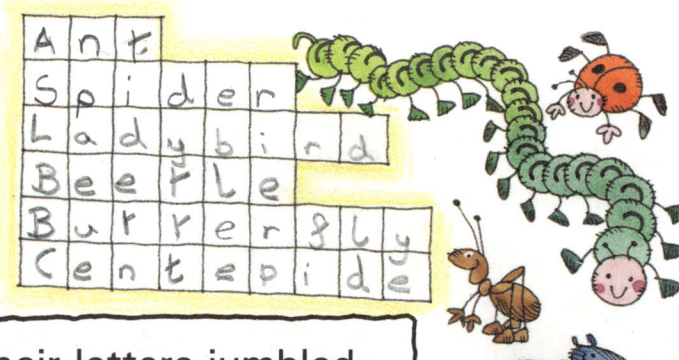

Ant
Spider
Ladybird
Beetle
Burrerfly
Centepide

Words with their letters jumbled are called **anagrams**.

CODES

a	b	c	d	e	f	g	h	i	j	k	l	m	n	o	p	q	r	s	t	u	v	w	x	y	z
z	y	x	w	v	u	t	s	r	q	p	o	n	m	l	k	j	i	h	g	f	e	d	c	b	a

Work out what this says:

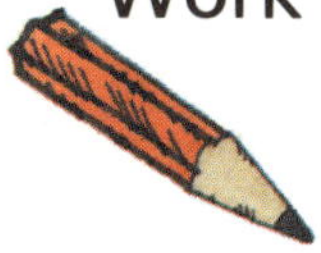

gsrh rh z evib hrnkov xlwv

....

Now solve this code to find the animal names.

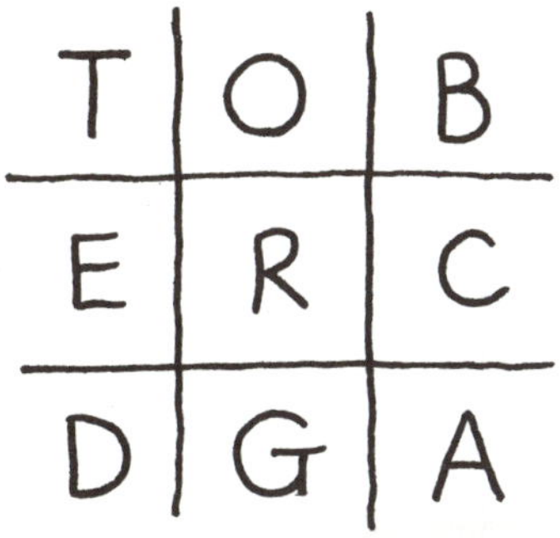
T O B
E R C
D G A

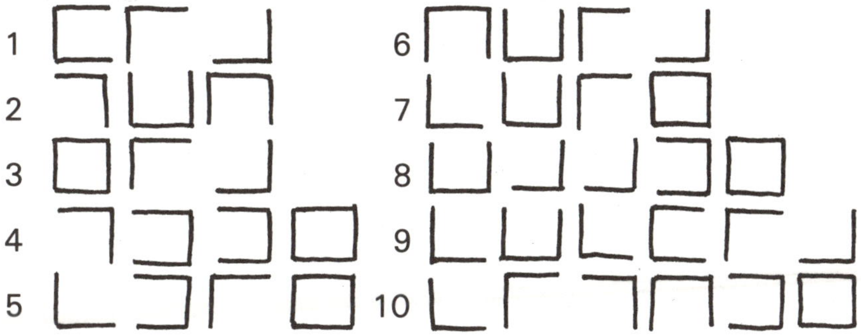
1
2
3
4
5
6
7
8
9
10

Make up some more codes.

SENTENCES

RULE Sentences start with a **capital letter** and end with a **full stop**.

Sort out these mixed up sentences.

1 was tall. The policeman
2 for you. Apples are good
3 on your Hair grows head.
4 seven days There are week. in a

Put the correct number by each sentence.
Make up your own sentence for number 6.

☐ The cat chased the mouse.   ☐ The cat woke up.
☐ It tripped over the cat's whiskers.   ☐ The mouse crept past.
[1] The cat sat on the mat.   [6] _____

RULE Questions start with a **capital letter** and end with a **question mark**.

Sort out these mixed up questions.

| is What name? your | _____ | me? Do like you | _____ |
| you are Where going? | _____ | When you write? will | _____ |

Which questions did the girl ask the witch?
Remember the ?. Choose the words from her hat.

I am the witch of the North.
How __fast__ can you __fly__?
I can fly at 100 kilometres an hour.
What __is__ __your__ favourite __food__?
I like chips cooked in my cauldron.

(Who are you?)

Look closely at this picture.
Are these sentences **true** or **false**?

1 There are five squares.   __true__
2 There is one small circle.   __true__
3 A big blue square has a cross inside.   __false__
4 There are three red triangles.   __false__

Write the question to go with each answer.

1 __what rests on two triangles.__
1 The rectangle rests on two triangles.
2 __What is between two squares__
2 The large circle is between two squares.

NOUNS, ADJECTIVES, VERBS

Nouns are words used for people, places and things, for example, *farmer, garage, book*.

Names are called **proper nouns** and start with a capital letter, for example, *John, New York*.

Sort out these nouns under the correct heading.

eagle plaice potato France cod robin carrots Rome onions England sparrow sardine

VEGETABLES	BIRDS	FISH	PLACES
potato carrots onions	eagle robin sparrow	plaice cod sardine	France Rome England

Adjectives tell us more about nouns.
Colour words are adjectives.
Pick an adjective to make these nouns more interesting.

fierce dog
narrow boat
thin man
green apple
sharp teeth
hot sun

thin fierce
green narrow
sharp hot

Verbs tell us what is being done.

Fill in the missing verbs.

jogging   climbing   weight-lifting
rowing   skipping

Nina is ___weight___ ___
Shameen is _____
Michael is _____
Tim is _____
Clare is _____

We need **nouns**, **verbs** and **adjectives** to make **sentences**.

Keep fit Club

Here is a nonsense sentence.

Green monkeys like hairy frogs.

Make up some funny sentences of your own and draw pictures. Don't forget the capital letters and full stops.

Choose the noun, verb or adjective to complete these sentences.

1 The ___man___ (man, banana, clock) swam

   in the ___sea___ (bath, sea, road).

2 The girl ___read___ (ate, read, liked) her book.

3 The ___fierce___ (blue, silly, fierce) dog bit the man's leg.

TRICKY WORDS

there / their

These words sound the same but are spelt differently.

there = **place**
 I sit there.

their = **belonging to**
 Their eyes are blue.

Fill in the missing words.

T_____ is a strange planet. Weird creatures live t_____. T_____ three legs and t_____ flat feet help them to walk on t_____ planet. They have no noses because t_____ planet smells.

where / were

Remember:
where has **here** inside
(Think of a place.)

were has **we** inside
(We were doing something.)

Fill in the missing words.

W_____ are your mice, John?

They w_____ under my bed on Wednesday. They w_____ behind my books on Thursday. They w_____ in my boots on Friday. Now I don't know w_____ they are!

CROSSWORDS

Picture clues

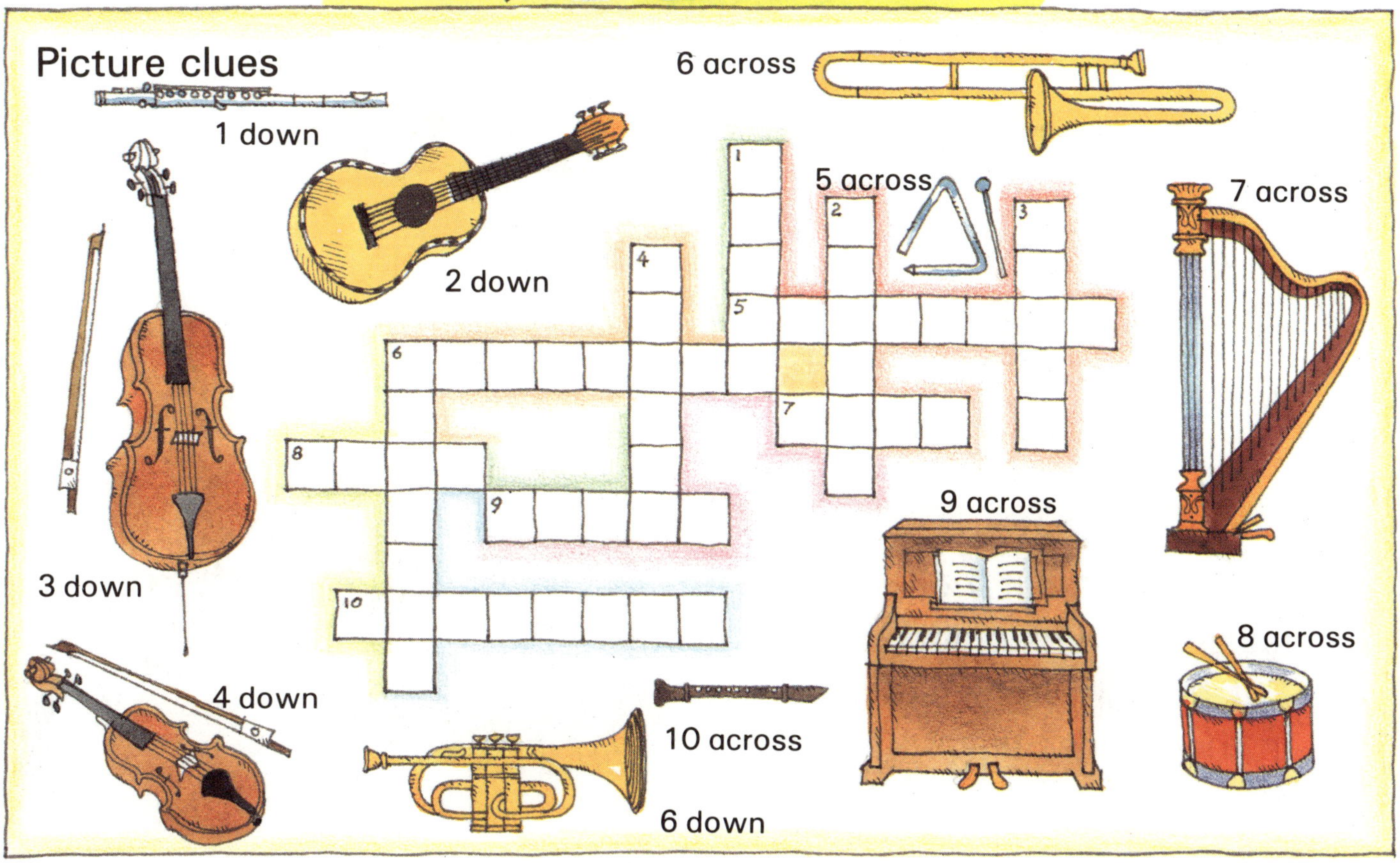

- 1 down (flute)
- 2 down (guitar)
- 3 down (cello)
- 4 down (violin)
- 5 across (triangle)
- 6 across (trombone)
- 7 across (harp)
- 8 across (drum)
- 9 across (piano)
- 10 across (trumpet)
- 6 down (recorder)

Word clues

Down

1. Opposite of up.
2. The American flag is ____, white and blue.
4. It turns the bicycle wheels.
5. Teddy, dolls and train sets are all _____.
6. 5 + 5
9. Juicy, crisp fruit with red or green peel.
11. The girl _____ a question.
12. Grown up boys.
13. A tiny bit of water.
15. The piece which goes in the horse's mouth.

Across

1. Opposite of light.
3. A tiny round shape.
7. Third weekday.
8. A kitten grows into this.
10. A word meaning sick.
14. The ninth month.
16. A farmer sows this.
17. _____ at red lights.

SPELLING FIRST AID

To practise your spelling follow these steps.

| **LOOK** closely at the word. | **SAY** the word. | **COVER** the word with a piece of paper. | **WRITE** the word. | **CHECK** to see if you got it right. |

Try these:

- watch
- heart
- glove
- leopard

How many ticks did you get?

Lots of difficult words have letter patterns hidden inside. Put the **ight** letter pattern in the spaces below.

br _ _ _ _
r _ _ _ _
fl _ _ _ _
m _ _ _ _ y
l _ _ _ _ ning
f _ _ _ _
moonl _ _ _ _
midn _ _ _ _
del _ _ _ _

Use the words from your list to complete the story about the knight.

At midn_____ the kn_____ turned r_____.
The br_____ moonl_____ shone down on him.
There was a flash of l_____ning.
The kn_____ saw the m_____y dragon hiding.
There was a terrible f_____.
The dragon took fl_____.
The kn_____ smiled with del_____.

Write the **ould** letter pattern in the spaces.

w_____ _____
sh_____ _____
c_____ _____
w_____n't _____
c_____n't _____

NOW~LOOK, SAY, COVER, WRITE, CHECK.

Write the **ice** letter pattern on each iceberg.

m___   n___   ___ cream   pol___ ___ man

not ___

Can you think of any more **ice** words?

A RULE TO REMEMBER
i before **e** except after **c**

Now put the **ie** letter pattern inside the words in the pie.

p__ce   p__
t__   f__ld
bel__ve
f__rce   th__f

Find the **ie** words again in this puzzle.

a	e	b	e	l	i	e	v	e
f	h	t	i	e	o	u	w	t
p	i	e	a	e	i	o	u	s
f	i	e	l	d	x	p	c	l
a	c	t	h	i	e	f	w	c
o	p	u	f	i	e	r	c	e
p	i	e	c	e	p	s	a	w

WORD DETECTIVE

Some long words have little words hidden inside. Read these:

as   do   very   on   the   aid   hen   new   end

Now find them again in these longer words.

pretend   does   their   everyone   once   was   said   knew   when

Write each word again using

LOOK	SAY	COVER	WRITE	CHECK

How many ticks?

Find the word **ear** inside each word in the giant's **beard**. Use the words to complete these sentences.

1 I must l____n my tables off by h____t.

2 S____ch in the ____th for treasure.

3 ____ly this morning my father shaved off his b____d.

learn
beard
earth
early
search
heart

INSTRUCTIONS FOR THE GAMES AND PUZZLES ON THE CARD WHICH FOLLOWS ARE PRINTED ON THE INSIDE BACK COVER.

THE MAGIC OF E

Adding **e** to the end of some small words turns them into new words.

It turns a **cap** into a **cape** or a **fir** into a **fire**.

Try your own magic. How many new words can you make by adding **e** to the end of smaller ones?

Some words have letters which we don't say when we read them. These are called **silent letters**.

Draw a circle round the silent letter in these words.

know   knit
comb   lamb
wrist wrong
climb write

Now write the words under the correct heading.

silent k	silent b	silent w

ONE OR MORE

SINGULAR means one of something.

RULE TO TURN A SINGULAR NOUN INTO A PLURAL NOUN WE OFTEN JUST ADD 'S'.

PLURAL means more than one.

Add **s** to make these **plural nouns**.

one apple : ten _____
a boy : four _____
an egg : a dozen _____

A dozen is 12!

RULE

Sometimes, if a word ends with **s** or **ss** or **x** or **ch** or **sh**, we need to add **es** to make the word plural.

a box → two_____

a dress → six_____

an atlas → three_____

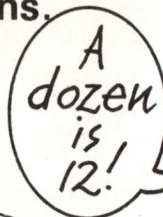

Look at a newspaper or a page in a book and make a list of more words like this.

RULE

Sometimes the noun stays the same. It is either *always* singular or *always* plural.

We talk of a **flock of sheep** NOT sheeps. And we'd look silly in a pair of trouser. It's a **pair of trousers**.

Think about these:
**fish
spectacles
aircraft**

Finish these sentences with the correct plural noun.

1 The _____ were late. (**bus, buses**)

2 This pair of _____ is blunt. (**scissors, scissor**)

3 The two _____ wore crowns. (**princess, princesses**)

4 Dan had three pet _____. (**frog, frogs**)

LOTS AND LOTS

There are many interesting **group words** for animals, people or things.

a pack of wolves

a herd of cattle

a swarm of insects

What do you think these group words are for?

A litter of ....

A shoal of ....

A bouquet of ....

A troop of ....

Find some more group words. Use a dictionary to help.

_____

_____

_____

_____

_____

HOW MANY?

Do you know the song *The Twelve Days of Christmas*?
This is what the man gave to his true love.

one partridge
two doves
three hens
four birds
five gold rings
six geese
seven swans
eight maids
nine ladies
ten lords
eleven pipers
twelve drummers

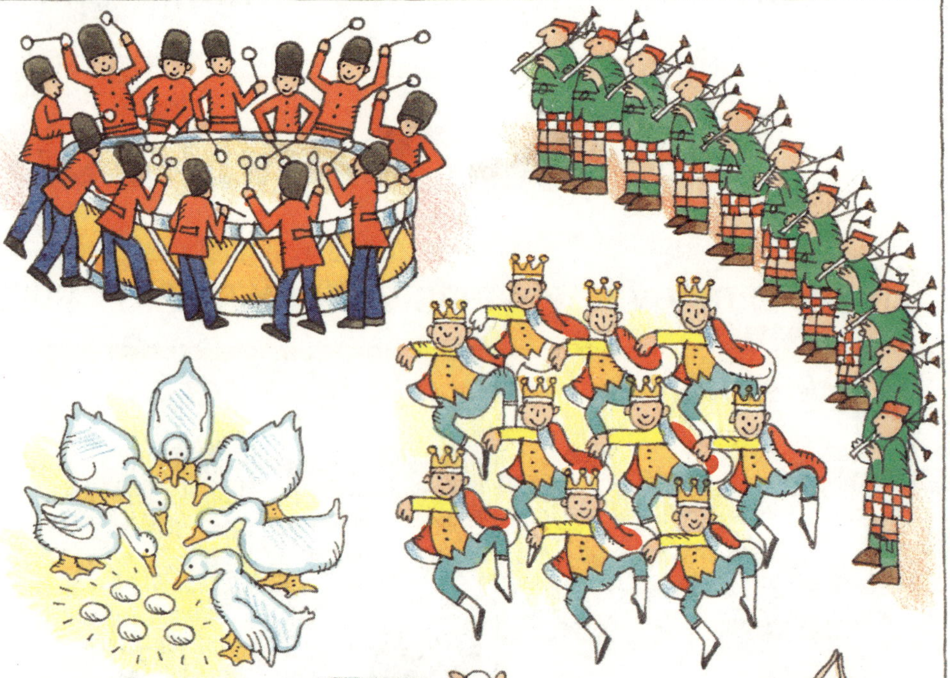

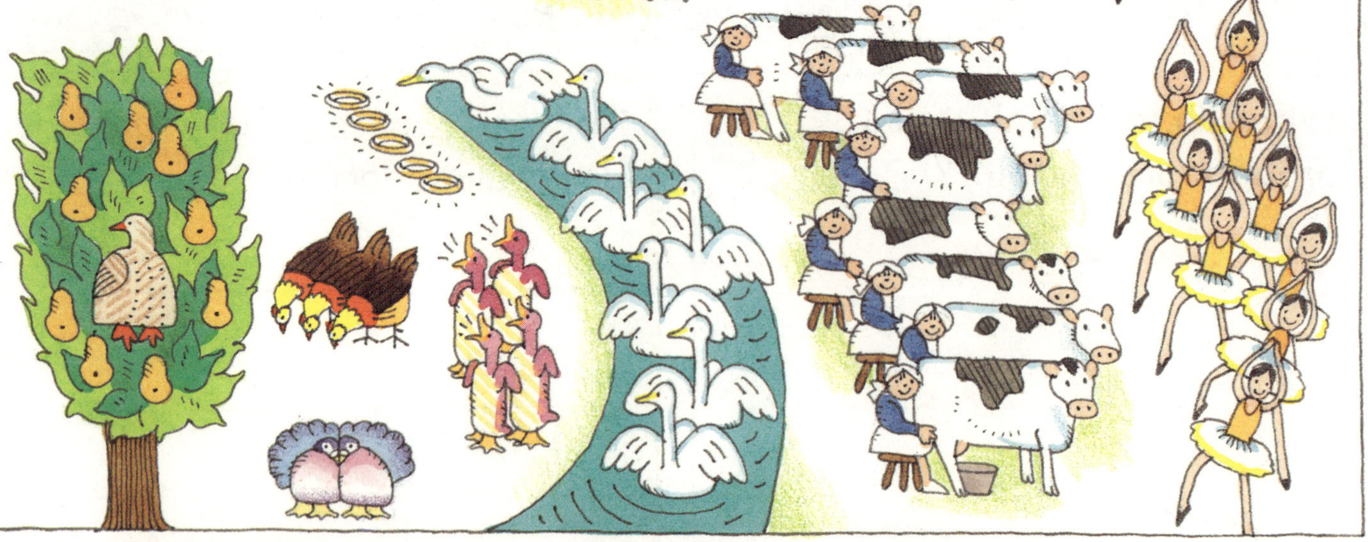

Use **LOOK** **SAY** **COVER** **WRITE** **CHECK**

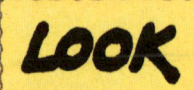

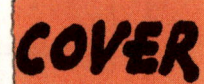

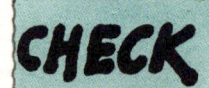

and fill in the number words below.

________________pipers ________________maids

________________swans ________________geese

________________birds ________________partridge

________________gold rings ________________drummers

DAYS OF THE WEEK

The names of the days of the week were written on the blackboard but the teacher has started to clean it. Fill in the missing letters.

M _ _ day
T _ _ _ day
We _ _ _ _ _ day
Th _ _ _ day
F _ _ day
Sa _ _ _ day
S _ _ day

Write the words again.

MONTHS OF THE YEAR

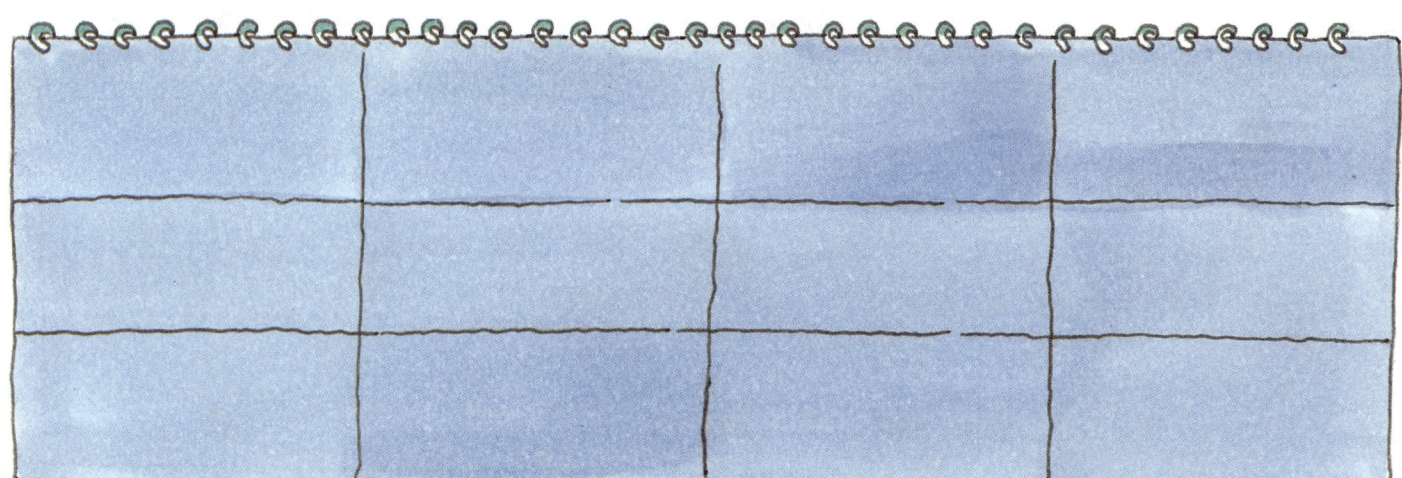

The names of the months have fallen off the calendar. Write them in the correct order.

MAY
SEPTEMBER
FEBRUARY
MARCH
APRIL
DECEMBER
NOVEMBER
JULY
JUNE
JANUARY
OCTOBER
AUGUST

GIVING INSTRUCTIONS

Instructions for making or doing something should be clear, simple and in the right order.
Match these instructions to the pictures for making a *Get Well* card.

1. Fold a piece of coloured card in half.
2. Draw round a glass with a felt pen to make a circle on the front.
3. Draw eyes, a nose and a sad mouth for the face.
4. Draw arms and legs.
5. Draw a big bump on the head and stick a real plaster across it.
6. Write your message inside.

Imagine telling an alien how you clean your teeth.
Think of what you use and what you do in the correct order.
Write out your instructions.

_____
_____
_____
_____

GIVING DIRECTIONS

Tom the truck driver has to deliver a parcel. He has a map but he's lost the directions. Write some new directions to take him to the factory.

Directions
_____
_____
_____
_____
_____
_____

SAME OR DIFFERENT

Many words have nearly the same meaning. These are called synonyms.
Knowing these can make your descriptions or stories more interesting.

These are synonyms.

small and little

fear and terror

Match these words to their synonyms.

help   old   round   hard   copy

smell   riches   strange

ancient _____
odour _____
aid _____
wealth _____
difficult _____

peculiar _____
imitate _____
circular _____

Use a dictionary to help you!

tall and short

fat and thin

Now find the words which mean the **opposite** of those below.

clean _____
bad _____
new _____
alive _____

empty _____
slow _____
strong _____
night _____

PROVERBS

Proverbs are wise sayings!

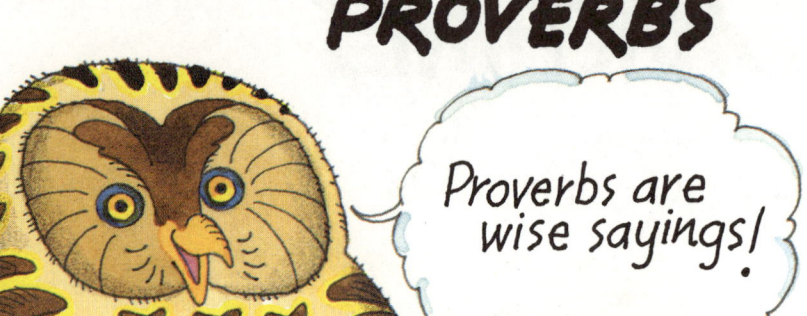

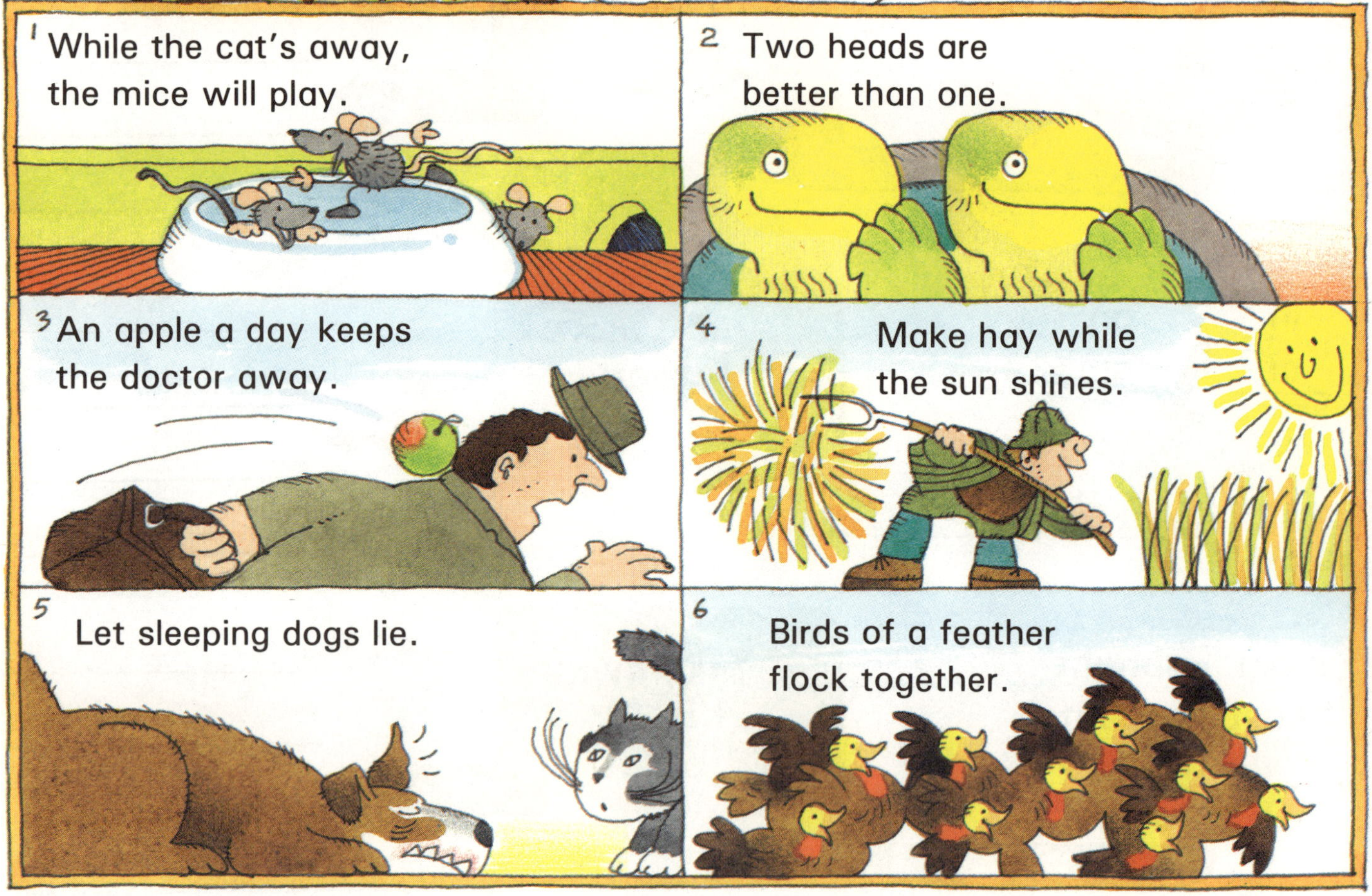
1 While the cat's away, the mice will play.
2 Two heads are better than one.
3 An apple a day keeps the doctor away.
4 Make hay while the sun shines.
5 Let sleeping dogs lie.
6 Birds of a feather flock together.

What is the *real* meaning of the proverbs?
Write the number by the correct meaning.

People who think or do things in the same way often stay together. ☐
When something is over or finished, leave it alone. ☐
Two people talking together can solve a problem. ☐
Work today. Tomorrow things might go wrong. ☐
Eating fresh fruit is good for your health. ☐
While Mum and Dad are out, the children might be naughty. ☐

Make a list of more proverbs and their meanings.

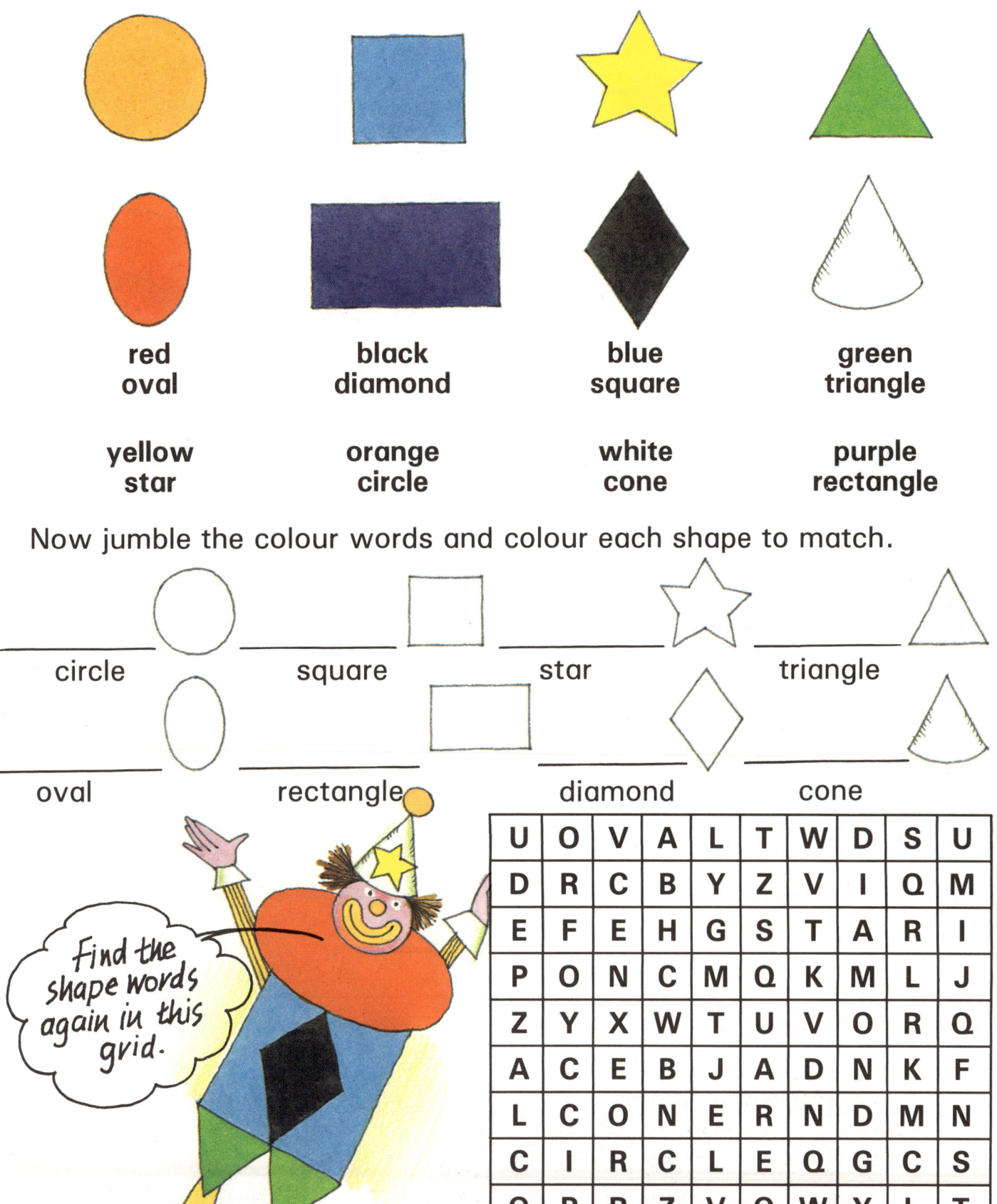

GIVE YOURSELF A TEST!

Find some paper and give yourself 20 minutes to do the test.

REMEMBER – to test your spelling use –

LOOK
SAY
COVER
WRITE
CHECK

① Spell these words:
friend   when   tired   thought   was   their   every
because   said   where

② Write out the small words hidden inside these words.
there   some   were   once   knew

③ Write 4 words which need a capital letter.

④ Write 2 sentences. Remember the rules!

⑤ Write 4 nouns.

⑥ Write 4 adjectives to go with the 4 nouns.

⑦ Write 4 verbs which say what you do when you go to bed.

⑧ Write out the alphabet.
Now put these words in alphabetical order.
helicopter   hear   pretty   shout
pretend   school   ship   victory

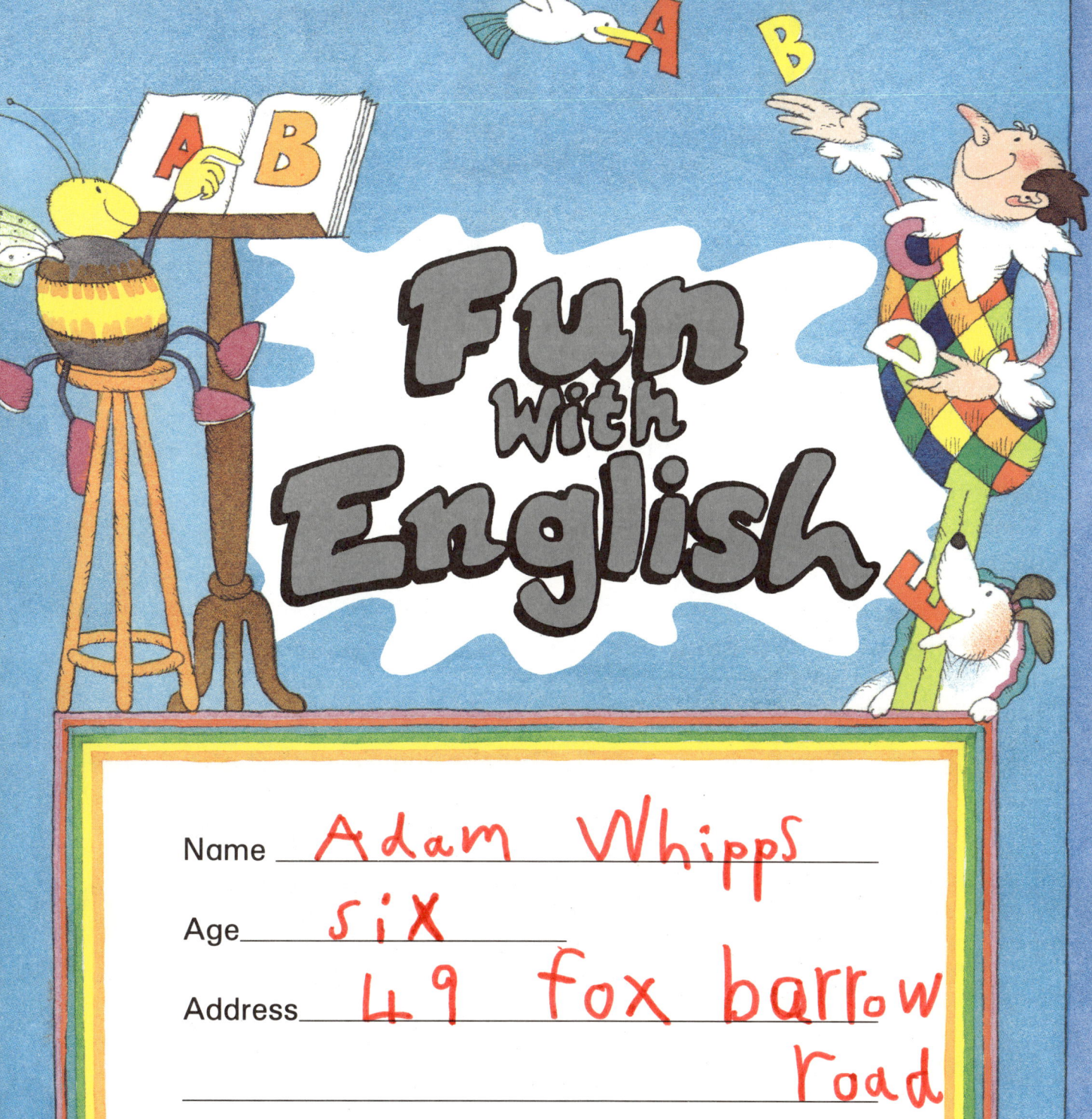

Fun with English

Name: Adam Whipps
Age: six
Address: 49 fox barrow road

by Kay Hiatt
designed and illustrated by John Lobban

Ladybird Books

ALPHABETICAL ORDER

| Aa | Bb | Cc | Dd | Ee | Ff | Gg | Hh | Ii | Jj | Kk | Ll | Mm |
| Nn | Oo | Pp | Qq | Rr | Ss | Tt | Uu | Vv | Ww | Xx | Yy | Zz |

Here are the 26 letters of the alphabet, in order.
Telephone directories, dictionaries and even your school registers are all listed in alphabetical order.

Write your name here: _____

Now write it again, putting the letters in alphabetical order.

_____

In this race, Angela is in Lane 1. Put the rest in alphabetical order.

___ ANGELA
___ DANIEL
___ LOUISE
___ RAJESH
___ KATE
___ LORNA
___ ROGER
___ DONNA

Did you have trouble with Daniel and Donna or Louise and Lorna?

HINT
If the first letter is the same, look at the second letter. If that is the same, look at the third and so on.

Sort these words into alphabetical order.

taxi
ring

bird
toad

rose
bat